Coping™

COPING WITH

BIPOLAR DISORDER

Sherri Mabry Gordon

Rosen
YA™
New York

Published in 2020 by The Rosen Publishing Group, Inc.
29 East 21st Street, New York, NY 10010

First Edition

Library of Congress Cataloging-in-Publication Data

Names: Gordon, Sherri Mabry, author.
Title: Coping with bipolar disorder / Sherri Mabry Gordon.
Description: New York : Rosen Publishing, 2020. | Series: Coping | Audience: Grades 7–12. | Includes bibliographical references and index.
Identifiers: LCCN 2018050662| ISBN 9781508187462 (library bound) | ISBN 9781508187455 (paperback)
Subjects: LCSH: Manic-depressive illness—Juvenile literature.
Classification: LCC RC516 .G665 2020 | DDC 616.89/5—dc23
LC record available at https://lccn.loc.gov/2018050662

Manufactured in China

For many of the images in this book, the people photographed are models. The depictions do not imply actual situations or events.

CONTENTS

INTRODUCTION

Abraham Lincoln, Vincent van Gogh, Winston Churchill—the list of famous people who may have suffered from bipolar disorder is extensive. In fact, bipolar disorder impacts approximately 5.7 million people in the United States every year, or 2.6 percent of people eighteen and older, according to the Depression and Bipolar Support Alliance. Yet, there is still so much to learn about this mental health disorder. Too often, people have a fear of bipolar disorder. They assume that a person will constantly behave in ways that are unpredictable and scary—that people with bipolar disorder are dangerous, violent, or can snap at any given moment.

These stereotypes are hurtful and far from the truth. While extreme manic phases may cause people with bipolar disorder to do outlandish things, people struggling with bipolar disorder are so much more than their condition. And if their illness is managed effectively, they can live happy, productive lives.

If you or a loved one was recently diagnosed with bipolar disorder, you might feel frightened, alone, and even uncertain about the future. But getting a

While painting some of the best-known and most influential paintings in the world, many historians believe Vincent van Gogh also was battling symptoms of bipolar disorder.

5

diagnosis is good news. In fact, most people with bipolar disorder suffer with the condition for ten or more years before receiving an accurate diagnosis. Now, though, you or your loved one can receive the needed treatment.

The key to living with bipolar disorder is not to feel guilty, blame yourself, or feel ashamed. Bipolar

disorder is an illness and not a sign of weakness. There is nothing anyone did to cause the illness. Just like diabetes or any other health condition, it will need to be managed. But this can be done if the person afflicted with the illness follows a treatment plan monitored by a doctor.

One challenge in treating bipolar disorder is that people with bipolar disorder are often not consistent in taking their

Although the diagnosis of bipolar disorder did not exist during Abraham Lincoln's time, experts believe he may have suffered from the illness. He displayed periods of elation and depression.

medications. Going on and off medications, or not taking them at all, can lead to cycling through manic and depressive states. This then sets the person back in his or her efforts to get better. Too often, people with bipolar disorder start to feel better—or maybe they miss the way they feel during the manic phases—and they stop taking their medications all

When it comes to treating bipolar disorder, the key to feeling better is maintaining a consistent treatment plan. Those battling the disorder should follow their doctor's instructions.

together. But the thing to remember is that if a person is feeling better, it is likely due to the treatment plan. Every effort to maintain a consistent treatment plan is the key to managing bipolar disorder. Taking medications inconsistently can only complicate recovery.

Sure, living with bipolar disorder is not easy and can be tough, but by learning all you can about the illness, you or your family member can focus on the future. In fact, the sooner you or your family member learns to accept the diagnosis, the sooner you can find the right path, an effective treatment plan, and explore new opportunities. Remember, bipolar disorder doesn't have to control your life or your loved one's life. You may not be able to change the diagnosis, but you can change how you view it and how to manage it.

CHAPTER ONE

Overview of Bipolar Disorder

In 2010, pop star Demi Lovato's life seemed to be unraveling. She was addicted to drugs, struggling with an eating disorder, and cutting herself to get a release from all the pain she was feeling. Her life was spiraling out of control, and she had no idea what was at the root of her problems. Of course, the bullying she experienced as a kid was a contributing factor, but there was something much deeper at the core. She just didn't know what.

After an altercation with a band member while on tour, Lovato was forced to confront the issues that were plaguing her. Her family and management team held an intervention, and she checked into a rehab facility to address her addiction as well as her bulimia and cutting.

In 2010, Demi Lovato was diagnosed with bipolar disorder after a string of negative events led to her hospitalization. Her loved ones were determined to get her the help she needed.

"They sat me down and said, 'You can't live like this,'" Lovato tells ABC News's Robin Roberts. While in treatment, Lovato not only learned to change her coping skills, but was also diagnosed with bipolar disorder. She says it was a relief to finally have an explanation for her struggles.

"I had no idea that I [had bipolar disorder] until I went into treatment," Lovato tells Roberts. "I was actually manic a lot of the times that I would take on workloads, and I would say, yes, I can do this, I can do this. I was conquering the world, but then I would come crashing down, and I would be more depressed than ever."

For years, people told Lovato she was simply depressed. Even she didn't understand what was happening with her. Sometimes she would be upset and other times she would have

For years, Demi Lovato did not know why she felt the way she did. As a result, she turned to drugs, alcohol, and cutting as a way to self-medicate and to try to feel better.

periods of intense energy, where she felt she could accomplish anything. In fact, she would often stay up until 5 a.m. and write seven songs in one night.

"Sometimes I felt invincible, and it was these moments when my mind would go all over the place," she says in an article by Christina Heiser in *Women's Health*. These feelings also led to her addiction.

"When you don't know what's happening, why you're feeling certain ways, and you don't have the answers yet, people tend to self-medicate, which is exactly what I did," she says. Lovato now focuses on her treatment plan, thanks to her team and support system. She uses these tools to maintain her sobriety.

Today, Lovato is still working to manage her mental illness, her addictions, and her eating disorder. She admits the road is challenging, but she is working at it every single day.

Understanding Bipolar Disorder

According to the National Institute of Mental Health (NIMH), bipolar disorder is a serious brain illness that causes people to go through unusual mood changes. Typically, bipolar disorder is characterized by unusual shifts in mood, energy, and activity levels. It also impacts a person's ability to carry out day-to-day tasks. These mood changes are different from the normal ups and downs that everyone goes through. Usually, they are more extreme. They can also impact job and school performance and often leave damaged relationships in their wake.

Overall, the moods that people with bipolar disorder experience range from feeling extremely up, elated, and energized to very sad, down, and hopeless. The up periods are known as the manic episodes and the down periods are known as depressive episodes. Sometimes the symptoms of bipolar disorder are so severe that the person with the illness cannot function properly. As a result, he or she is unable to do what is expected at home, at school, or at work.

Typically, bipolar disorder develops when people are in their late teens or early adult years. In fact, at least half of all cases start before the person reaches age twenty-five, according to the NIMH. Still, there are exceptions to this. Some people will have their first symptoms in childhood and in others, the disorder does not show up until late in life.

Why You Should Never Call Someone Bipolar

Demi Lovato has been a consistent advocate for good mental health. She wants people with mental illness to know that it is possible "to live well, feel well and find happiness," she says in *Women's Health*. As a result, she has been an outspoken advocate. She is also the spokesperson for the campaign Be Vocal. This program focuses on encouraging people with mental illness to speak up. The goal is to change the way mental illness is talked about. They want to break down the stigma surrounding it.

In fact, when it comes to bipolar disorder, Lovato says a lot of people do not understand it. Her goal is to change that. At the top of her list is how the word "bipolar" is used. Too many times, people will say "she is bipolar" instead of "she has bipolar disorder." What's more, people often use the word "bipolar" as an insult. For instance, they might say "he is so bipolar" or "the weather is bipolar." These statements are hurtful to someone who has the illness. It is the same as saying "that is so gay." Not only does it show a lack of understanding, but it is also extremely hurtful.

"We shouldn't be using…a brain disorder to insult someone," writes Suzannah Weiss in *Teen Vogue*. "Your mental and physical health aren't flaws. They're just part of who you are—and they're definitely nothing to be ashamed of."

Lovato agrees. She feels that people should not be defined by their mental illness. And, she certainly does not want to be defined by hers.

"I think when people refer to me as being bipolar, it's something that's true—I am bipolar—but I don't like people to use it as a label. . . . It's something that I have, it's not who I am," she tells Teen Vogue.

Type of Bipolar Disorder

There are four basic types of bipolar disorder. They all involve clear changes in mood, energy, and activity levels but differ in how they manifest and in how extreme the changes are.

Bipolar I disorder is defined by manic episodes that last at least seven days or by manic symptoms that are so severe that the person needs immediate care in a hospital setting. Typically, depressive episodes occur as well and can last two weeks. Mixed episodes are possible where a person will experience both mania and depression at the same time.

Bipolar II disorder is less severe than bipolar I. Instead, the person experiences a pattern of depressive episodes as well as hypomanic episodes. Hypomania is not as severe as mania. It still causes issues in a person's life and is recognizable by others but is not as extreme as mania.

Cyclothymic disorder, which is also known as cyclothymia, involves numerous periods of hypomanic episodes and depressive episodes lasting for at least two years (one year for children and teens). Overall, cyclothymia is a mood disorder that is a milder bipolar disorder. While a person with cyclothymic disorder has moods that swing between short periods of mild depression and hypomania, they never reach the severity or duration of a major depressive episode or a full mania episode.

Unspecified bipolar disorder contains all the symptoms of bipolar disorder, but the episodes and behaviors do not match the three types listed above. Doctors sometimes use this classification for patients who display behaviors that are consistent with bipolar disorder but fall short of the criteria needed to make a definite diagnosis.

Why Diagnosing Bipolar Disorder Is So Hard

Getting a diagnosis of bipolar disorder takes time. In fact, it takes an average of six years for a person with bipolar disorder to get properly diagnosed, according to Bipolar Hope, an online resource for people with bipolar disorder. Part of the issue is the fact that bipolar disorder often occurs simultaneously alongside other illnesses and conditions. This is called comorbidity. Some illnesses and conditions that often exist alongside bipolar disorder include anxiety, ADHD, borderline personality disorder, substance abuse, and eating disorders. Also, people with bipolar disorder are more likely to experience thyroid issues, hormonal changes, obesity, diabetes, and heart issues.

Half of all people with bipolar disorder will see at least three mental health professionals before getting a correct diagnosis according to a survey by the National Depressive and Manic-Depressive Association, writes Jennifer Thomas in *Health* magazine. What's more, about 40 percent of people with the illness are initially diagnosed with major depression, Dr. S. Nassir Ghaemi, the director of the Mood Disorders Program at Tufts Medical Center in Boston, told Thomas.

Dr. Ghaemi says there are several reasons for the confusion. First, many people with bipolar disorder experience depression before mania, and it is the depression that leads people to get medical help. Consequently, many people have never actually experienced a manic episode. So, there are no signs or symptoms to point to. Second, when people do experience mania, many have no idea what is going on. They may think they just have a lot of energy or passion for life.

Often, to diagnose bipolar disorder, mental health professionals need the help of family members.

When diagnosing bipolar disorder, it can help to have family members attend medical appointments. They can provide info about behaviors the patient may not realize or remember.

They can share details about any suspected mania or hypomania, a milder form of mania that is much less noticeable. Overall, it takes time and effort to accurately diagnose bipolar disorder and many times people just want a quick answer rather than exploring all the possibilities.

Take a Walk in Their Shoes

It is no secret that bipolar disorder is a confusing illness—both for the person living with it and for someone on the outside looking in. What's more, people with bipolar disorder are often reluctant to talk about how the illness makes them feel. Many times, they feel shame and guilt for having bipolar disorder, especially when they see how it impacts other people. For this reason, it is important to understand what it feels like to live with bipolar disorder. Once you do, you will be able to empathize with the person as well as make sense of their behavior and get them help when they need it.

Manic Episodes

During a manic episode, a person with bipolar disorder will be full of energy and maybe even bouncing off the walls. Sometimes this manic phase makes the person look like a happy, upbeat, fun, and optimistic person—someone who is the life of the party and great to be around. Other times, you may notice erratic behaviors like excessive talking, speaking really quickly, being easily distracted, and acting impulsively.

A thirty-year-old California man describes his manic episodes to HealthLine:

During a mania episode, I have tons of energy and don't want to stop. Unfortunately, this is [also] when I go out more, spend all

During a manic episode, a person with bipolar disorder may appear extremely energetic, talk really fast, and want to take risks. People experiencing mania can also be self-destructive.

21

my money, and drink too much. I [also] feel like I can do anything, so my self-worth skyrockets...but when the mania burns out, I've got nothing left.

Depressive Episodes

When someone with bipolar disorder experiences a depressive episode, he or she could be laughing and having fun one day and then the next, that person seems to withdraw completely from life. He or she isolates himself or herself, seems to be really irritated, struggles to get out of bed, and experiences difficulties in meeting his or her obligations or responsibilities. When this happens, that person is experiencing a depressive episode.

The Californian man explains to his depressive episodes to HealthLine:

When I am depressed, I want to be left alone. It's not that I want to be by myself; I want everyone to disappear. I don't want to go anywhere, see anyone, or do anything. It's like no matter what I do, people are telling me I'm doing something wrong.

A depressive episode can make someone with bipolar disorder feel overcome with hopelessness. He also may cry a lot, become irritable, or refuse to do things he once loved to do.

Stability

Although bipolar disorder is characterized by two very different moods, or polar opposite moods, there are times when a person with bipolar disorder will experience a more stable mood. For the man

23

from California mentioned earlier, this is the time that he imagines what life is like for everyone else. He describes this stable time to HealthLine:

> *I wake up in the morning and I feel fine. I enjoy the little things, and I'm not loathing the future...I honestly wish I could stay in this mindset all the time, but I know that won't happen. I've accepted that my moods will change on their own.*

Myths & **FACTS**

Today, people have a basic understanding of bipolar disorder due to awareness campaigns. Yet, there are still myths about the condition that many people believe. Here is a closer look at the top myths surrounding bipolar disorder.

Myth: Bipolar disorder is just a fancy name for mood swings.

Fact: While bipolar disorder is a mood disorder, the mood swings associated with the illness are very different from the mood swings someone without the disorder might experience. In general, the mood swings that people with bipolar disorder experience are severe and interfere with the person's day-to-day activities.

Myth: The only way to treat bipolar disorder is with drugs.

Fact: It is true that certain drugs are an important part of managing bipolar disorder, but they are only one part of an effective treatment plan. For instance, people with bipolar disorder also benefit from counseling, or talk therapy, as well

(continued on the next page)

(continued from the previous page)

as engaging in aerobic exercise, eating healthy, and maintaining a consistent sleep schedule.

Myth: People experiencing a manic episode are happy and having fun.

Fact: Everyone experiences bipolar disorder differently. For some people, the manic phase is enjoyable. They like the feeling of being invincible and having lots of energy. But for other people, it is a really frightening time because they lose their impulse control. In fact, some people will feel edgy and irritable during a manic episode. Additionally, there is a lot of guilt after a manic phase because people will look back and see how much it disrupted their lives or hurt the people they love.

Recognizing Bipolar Disorder in Yourself and Others

For seventeen years, Mariah Carey kept her diagnosis of bipolar disorder a secret. Instead of talking about it or letting others know what she was going through, she says she lived in denial, fear, and isolation. Her reasoning? She was afraid that she would lose everything. She also didn't want to believe it was true, or worse yet allow it to define her.

"I didn't want to carry around a stigma of a lifelong disease that would define me and potentially end my career," Carey tells *People* editor-in-chief, Jess Cagle. "I was so terrified of

For more than a decade, Mariah Carey kept the fact that she has bipolar disorder a secret. She was afraid the stigma around the mental illness would cause her to lose all she'd worked hard for.

losing everything, I convinced myself the only way to deal with this was to not deal with this."

But now Carey is being more open about her illness. She hopes that doing so will give others more understanding into what it means to live with bipolar disorder. She wants to eliminate the stigma around mental health issues.

Carey tells *People* magazine:

I'm in a really good place right now, where I'm comfortable discussing my struggles with bipolar II disorder. I'm hopeful we can get to a place where the stigma is lifted from people... [Bipolar disorder] can be incredibly isolating. [But] it does not have to define you and I refuse to allow it to define me or control me.

Living in Denial

Perhaps one of the most difficult things about bipolar disorder is that the people who have this mental health issue are often unwilling to accept that something is wrong with them. They do not want to believe that the diagnosis is accurate. Instead, just like Carey, they live in denial, fear, and isolation. In fact, 50 percent of people with bipolar disorder refuse help and still live with the symptoms, according to Julie Fast, a mental health expert and contributor to the website Bipolar Happens.

One reason people deny that they have the condition is that it is often too painful for them to accept. Imagine being told that you have a mental illness that will impact every aspect of your life and require you to make significant changes to your lifestyle. Too many times, people diagnosed with bipolar disorder find it easier to deny that there is a problem than to accept that they have a lifelong illness that will impact the way they think, feel, and behave. The thought of completely changing everything in their life in order to cope seems insurmountable at times.

Having a dual diagnosis also can contribute to denial. When someone has been given a dual diagnosis, this means that in addition to bipolar disorder, the person also struggles with a drug or alcohol addiction. In other words, if the person with bipolar disorder drinks or uses drugs, it may be hard for them to identify which symptoms are caused by the drugs, and which are from the bipolar disorder. Also, if they admit to having bipolar disorder, then they also will have to address their addictions. And for many people that is just simply too much to ask.

Another contributing factor in denial is the mania a person with bipolar disorder experiences. When he or she is having a manic episode, this changes the way a person thinks. He or she can become unreasonable and dangerous. What's more, many people believe that the mania makes them more creative and productive. They fear treating the condition will hinder their capabilities. But that is simply not true. Consequently, it is important that friends and family members know how to recognize the signs of a manic episode before it goes too far.

How to Recognize the Signs of Bipolar Disorder

Bipolar disorder is extremely hard to diagnose. In fact, many of the symptoms that people with bipolar disorder experience also can be caused by other conditions. What's more, it is not uncommon for doctors and other health care professionals to see a person's symptoms as separate issues and miss the real issue completely. Instead, they may assume the person is moody and difficult to work with.

"Chalking it up to moodiness or trouble at work or tiredness is pretty common," Carrie Bearden, PhD, told Tammy Worth for *Health*. "The disorder varies in severity." Dr. Bearden is an associate professor in residence at the David Geffen School of Medicine at UCLA.

What's more, if a person with bipolar disorder does seek help, it's usually when he or she is in a depressive state. As a result, it is not uncommon for that person to first be diagnosed with depression.

Common Signs of Mania or Hypomania

If you think that you, a friend, or a family member may have bipolar disorder, it is important to watch for specific indicators of the illness. Here are some of the signs to be on the lookout for.

- Requires less sleep or may not sleep at all
- Has lots of energy
- Talks very quickly
- Seems to bounce all over the place (both thoughts and actions)
- Has an elevated mood
- Becomes easily distracted or finds it hard to concentrate
- Appears restless, agitated, or irritated
- Is more self-confident or has a sense of self-importance
- Displays impulsiveness, makes poor decisions, or takes risks

Those experiencing a manic episode are often distractible, with pressured thoughts and rapid speech. To family and friends, they may not seem like themselves.

- Thinks very quickly and seems to have racing thoughts
- Has heightened senses and notices things like smells, colors, textures, and more
- Pursues goals, passions, and other interests

Keep in mind that manic episodes are extremely disruptive to people's lives. Dr. Kevin Gilliland,

33

a clinical psychologist, told Julie Mazziotta for *People* magazine:

> *When people have mania, their thoughts are often pressured, their speech is rapid, they may be more talkative. In the most severe cases, their need for sleep dramatically reduces, and they may go for a couple days or nights without much sleep at all, yet feel very rested with a lot of energy—and you shouldn't feel that way.*
>
> *It's [also] difficult to be around someone with mania. They're extremely distractible, and they get hyper-focused on a goal or project that is typically very different from their usual life.*

Common Signs of a Depressive Episode

A depressive episode is the polar opposite of a manic episode. Hence, the name bipolar disorder. Here are some things to watch for when it comes to depressive episodes.

- Becomes anxious or worries a lot
- Turns down offers to spend time with friends

- Loses interest in doing things they normally enjoy
- Is tearful, sad, or cries a lot
- Displays sleep issues, including sleeping too much or not being able to sleep at all
- Complains of being tired, fatigued, or that their body hurts
- Forgets things and doesn't follow through on responsibilities
- Has trouble completing tasks and frequently feels overwhelmed

Finally, some people with bipolar disorder may suffer from "mixed mania." In other words, they experience both mania and depression at the same time. As a result, they are often very irritable and agitated. Overall, keep in mind that bipolar disorder is more than just being moody. Instead, the moods that people with bipolar disorder experience are out of character for them. They also are sometimes severe and interfere with their lives, their relationships, and their activities.

"We are all irritable or moody sometimes," Dr. Bearden says in *Health*. "But in people with bipolar disorder it often becomes so severe that it interferes

During a depressive episode, a person with bipolar disorder will often find it hard to get out of bed and go through his normal day-to-day routine. He is also at an increased risk of suicide.

with their relationships—especially if the person is saying, 'I don't know why I'm so irritable…I can't control it.'"

What Causes Bipolar Disorder?

Researchers do not know for sure how bipolar disorder forms, but it is likely a combination of several things. In fact, there are a number of factors that can contribute to the development of bipolar disorder, including genetics, environmental factors, and brain structure.

Genetics. Studies have shown that bipolar disorder tends to run in families. Consequently, researchers believe that people can have a genetic predisposition for bipolar disorder. In fact, more than two-thirds of people with bipolar disorder have at least one close relative with the illness or with major depression. This fact suggests that the illness is somewhat hereditary. As a result, scientists are looking to see if specific genes are abnormal in people with bipolar disorder. Meanwhile, there are several studies of identical twins. According to an article by Jennifer H. Barnett and Jordan W. Smoller in the scientific journal *Neuroscience*, these studies have shown that if one twin develops bipolar disorder, the other twin has a 40 percent chance of developing it as well. Because this occurs less than half of the time, this means that other factors contribute to the illness as well, since identical twins share all the same genes.

Brain function and structure. Some scientists believe that neurotransmitters in the brain, such as serotonin and dopamine, do not function properly in people with bipolar disorder. In some cases, there is too much of the chemicals and in others there is not enough. In short, researchers are fairly certain that neurotransmitters are at least part of the cause of bipolar disorder. Still, more research is needed to determine the exact role.

Alcohol, Drug Abuse, and Bipolar Disorder

Many people with bipolar disorder will drink when they are experiencing a manic episode. This is called self-medicating, and they often drink in order to slow themselves down. Meanwhile, when they are in a depressive state they will often turn to alcohol or drugs to try to improve their mood. In fact, about 50 percent of people with bipolar disorder also have a substance abuse problem, says Dr. Bearden.

Moreover, the Addiction Center reports "in a study of people with bipolar disorder, approximately 60 percent of them had some history of substance abuse." No one really knows why, but bipolar disorder tends to make people more likely to abuse substances like drugs and alcohol. Unfortunately, drugs and alcohol make bipolar symptoms worse. And, abuse of alcohol or drugs can even trigger the onset of bipolar disorder. In fact, the Addiction Center reports that even people with no history of mental health issues may develop bipolar disorder as a result of substance abuse.

There are also some initial studies that show that the brains of people with bipolar disorder are somewhat different from those without the condition. In fact, studies show a difference in brain size as well. Yet, brain imaging or scans still cannot be used to diagnose bipolar disorder. Additional research in this area will help scientists learn more about the condition and how to treat it more effectively.

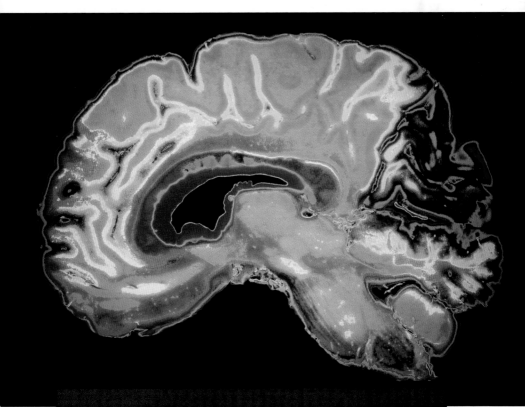

Even though brain scans cannot be used to diagnose bipolar disorder, initial studies show that people with bipolar disorder may have brains different in size from those without it.

Environmental factors. There are a number of outside factors that can also contribute to the development of bipolar disorder. For instance, abuse, mental stress, a significant loss, or some other traumatic event may contribute to or trigger bipolar disorder. Many researchers believe that people with a genetic predisposition for bipolar disorder may not have any noticeable symptoms until an environmental factor triggers the illness, and they experience their first severe mood swing.

All in all, if you, a friend, or a family member has bipolar disorder, the possibility of developing the disorder was probably there since birth and something triggered it. Until scientists can determine exactly what causes bipolar disorder and how to effectively treat it, they will keep searching for answers. But people with bipolar disorder should never assume that they are weak or that they caused it—instead they should remember that they have an illness. The good news is that it can be treated.

CHAPTER THREE

Treating Bipolar Disorder

Caitlyn Kalustian didn't know she was going through a bipolar episode until she was out of it. She didn't see the signs and didn't listen to those around her. In fact, if you asked her, she was doing fine. She was successful and happy—that is, until it all came crashing down, she writes in The Mighty, a digital health community for people facing health challenges and disabilities.

"That's the thing about mental illness. It often creeps," she explains. "Sometimes you can't feel the storm rolling in, reaching for you in dark wisps. Before you know it, you can't see anything."

Like Kalustian, people with bipolar disorder are often unaware that something is wrong. They may even enjoy their manic episodes. In fact, some have reported liking the increased energy levels as well as how crisp and vibrant the world appears to them. But mania can be very destructive because people experiencing an episode are more impulsive. During an episode, they may spend too much money, experiment with drugs, and be hurtful toward family and friends. And yet, they do not realize that there is anything wrong or know how to control it.

Kalustian explains:

> When I'm in an episode, it's like my brain and my mouth are not communicating. I hear myself saying these terrible things that spew out of my mouth like verbal diarrhea, but I can't stop them. The slightest [thing] sets me off and before I know it, there goes another relationship. Impulsivity rules my life. I think and feel, and then I act.

For this reason, it is very important for people with bipolar disorder to have a strong support network around them. They need people who understand their illness and can help them get help when they get off track. This group of people might include a combination of family, friends, counselors, and health care professionals that work as a team.

Why Treating Bipolar Disorder Is Important

It is important to remember that bipolar disorder is a lifelong illness with lots of ups and downs. But effective treatment can relieve most of the symptoms. Treatment also reduces the intensity of most manic episodes. Meanwhile, if left untreated, the ups and downs of the disorder can wreak havoc on a person's life.

For instance, the recurring depressive and manic episodes make it hard for the person to live a stable life. In the manic phase, the impulsive and erratic behaviors can cause a lot of damage. Meanwhile, the depressive phase makes it hard for the person to function. He or she may not want to get out of bed and find it hard to do anything at all.

When it comes to treating mental illnesses like bipolar disorder, though, most people don't know where to go when they need help. In fact, according to the National Alliance on Mental Illness, more than 60 percent of people with a mental illness

Statistics show that more than 60 percent of people won't seek treatment for a mental illness. But finding a mental health professional is the first step toward feeling better.

won't seek treatment in a given year. But it really needs to happen. The key is finding a mental health professional to diagnose the issue and then provide the professional help needed.

How Bipolar Disorder Is Treated

Most people think that all it takes to treat bipolar disorder is a simple prescription. But that is not the case. In fact, prescriptions are only one part of a good treatment plan. Monitoring bipolar disorder also requires regular counseling, a support system, and lifestyle changes like healthy eating, exercise, and a regular sleep schedule. It is also important for people with bipolar disorder to find healthy ways of coping with stress and challenges.

Once diagnosed, a person with the illness will likely need to see someone who specializes in treating bipolar disorder, like a psychiatrist or a psychologist. This person, or team of people, will help him or her find a prescription medication, or sometimes several medications, that work. The challenge is that everyone is different and responds differently to medications. Often people with bipolar disorder have to try several different medications before finding one that works. The key is to not give up. They need to work with their doctors until they find what works.

In the meantime, it is important that they put together a comprehensive treatment plan. According to International Bipolar Foundation (IBPF), the goal of any treatment plan is to relieve the symptoms and restore the person's ability to function normally. It also may address the problems that the illness has caused with family and friends or at work and school. The goal is to reduce the likelihood that these things reoccur. IBPF says there are five essential parts to a comprehensive treatment plan. These include:

1. **Medication.** Medications are the cornerstone of any effective treatment plan. These typically include mood-stabilizing drugs that help minimize the highs and lows of bipolar disorder. They also help keep symptoms under control.

2. **Psychotherapy.** Bipolar disorder often causes problems in a person's life. By working with a counselor, people with the illness can learn how to cope. They learn how to deal with

When someone with bipolar disorder works with a counselor, she learns to become aware of her triggers, or when things are starting to change. She can get help before an episode begins.

uncomfortable feelings, manage their stress, and regulate their moods. They also can learn how to mend broken relationships, apologize to friends and family, and take responsibility for the pain they may have caused.

3. **Education.** Learning about bipolar disorder not only helps people learn more about their condition, but it also helps them make wise decisions about their treatment. And, when they know more, they are less likely to experience setbacks or problems down the road.

4. **Support.** Dealing with bipolar disorder is not easy. For this reason, it is very important that people with the illness surround themselves with supportive people. These people should understand what they are dealing with and love them unconditionally. It also is helpful for people with bipolar disorder to join a support group. There, they can share their experiences with others who have the same condition. These people may be able to offer advice or encouragement.

5. **Lifestyle management.** By making and maintaining lifestyle changes, people with

bipolar disorder can keep mood episodes to a minimum. Some of the ways this is accomplished include getting consistent sleep, avoiding alcohol and drugs, exercising regularly, and minimizing stress. Even keeping sunlight exposure stable year-round has proven effective, according to IBPF.

Medications Used to Treat Bipolar Disorder

The medications used to treat bipolar disorder are powerful drugs designed to regulate moods and behaviors. As a result, they must be taken exactly as they are prescribed. Varying the doses, skipping days, or stopping the medication altogether can be very dangerous. Remember, there is no cure for bipolar disorder. It is a lifelong illness. As a result, when you are feeling good, it is important to remember that it is the medication doing its job. It is not an indication that you should stop taking your medications. In most people, maintaining a consistent treatment plan makes mania and depression happen less often. It also keeps changes in mood from being severe. For this

Bipolar disorder is treated with powerful drugs that should be taken as prescribed. Too often, people with bipolar disorder will feel better and stop taking their meds—that is never a good idea.

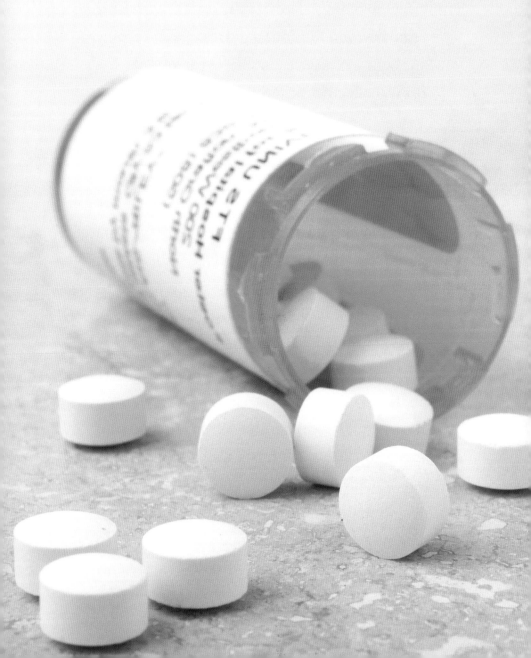

reason, it is very important for people with bipolar disorder to maintain a consistent treatment plan.

There are a number of medications used to help treat bipolar disorder. The problem is that finding the right combination often takes trial and error. Consequently, it is important to understand each medication that is prescribed and why it is needed. Understanding the reasons behind why the medication was prescribed reinforces why the medication is a necessary part of treatment. Or, if it does not make sense, then its use can be questioned.

The key is for the person with bipolar disorder to take an active role in the development of their treatment plan by becoming educated and asking questions. When he or she feels some ownership in his or her treatment plan, he or she is more likely to follow it. Here is an overview of some of the medications used to treat bipolar disorder.

Lithium. Since the 1960s, lithium has been the gold standard for treating bipolar disorder. It primarily treats mania but can also be used for bipolar depression, too. And it can be used for maintenance therapy, to prevent or reduce episodes from occurring. It is the only medication that has been proven to reduce the risk of suicide in people with bipolar disorder. Interestingly, lithium is a naturally occurring salt that can be used to manage mood symptoms. The downside is that it can create problems in the thyroid and the kidneys.

Anticonvulsants. Depakote is the most commonly prescribed anticonvulsant used to treat bipolar disorder. Even though it is used to treat seizures—and bipolar episodes are not seizures—it still is effective in some people. Although researchers are still studying why these drugs work, one theory is that they stabilize the neurons in the brain.

Antipsychotics. Originally developed to treat psychosis in schizophrenia, this group of medications can be effective in treating mania. The downside to these medications is that they can increase a person's risk of developing type II diabetes. They also may cause weight gain as well as high cholesterol. People on these medications may even develop tremors and stiffness.

Gene Testing May Make Treatments More Effective

Finding the right medication for someone with bipolar disorder often involves trial and error. For this reason, it can take years to find something that works. In the meantime, the person with the illness might experience ongoing mood changes, relapses, and difficulty functioning, along with side effects to the medications.

But there is new research that hopes to shorten the time it takes to find an effective treatment plan. The hope is that doctors will be able to find the correct prescriptions for people based on their genetic profile.

For instance, one study is focusing on the drug lithium, which is often considered the gold standard for treating bipolar disorder. Unfortunately, only about 30 percent of people with bipolar disorder will benefit from all that lithium can do, according to an article in The

(continued on the next page)

(continued from the previous page)

Conversation. Meanwhile, another 30 percent of people will get no benefit from the drug at all. And still others will require other medications to control the effects of the illness.

What researchers have discovered is that how a patient responds to lithium runs in families. This fact suggests that genetics, or heredity, play a role in the drug's effectiveness. As a result, researchers believe that people with bipolar disorder often have a "biological signature" that predicts how they will respond to different mood-stabilizing medications. Still, a lot of work needs to be done before these early discoveries can be used. But in the future, there may be tests that psychiatrists can do to determine what medicines will work. This provides hope for people with bipolar disorder and their families. In the future, finding the right medications may not take as long. And people with the illness can begin to feel better sooner.

Mood-boosting antidepressants. When most people think about bipolar disorder, they think of mania. But recurrent, severe depressive episodes can be just as disruptive to a person's life as mania.

What's more, depression is sometimes the first mood episode to show up. As a result, antidepressants are often the first medications prescribed. The issue is that bipolar depression is different from unipolar depression. As a result, bipolar disorder does not always respond well to antidepressants and can actually trigger a manic episode. Using antidepressants with bipolar disorder must be closely monitored by a doctor.

Sleeping pills and anxiolytics. Bipolar disorder often includes anxiety and sleeplessness as well. Consequently, it can be very hard for a person with the illness to calm down and get some sleep. As a result, your doctor may prescribe an antianxiety drug or a sleeping pill. Generally, these are not prescribed long term because they can be addictive.

Remember, the key to treating bipolar disorder is early detection. Not only does it allow the person with the illness a better chance of getting well and staying well, but it also can prevent things from spiraling out of control. In fact, with proper treatment, people with bipolar disorder can live happy and productive lives. The first step is recognizing that they need help getting better.

Mike Bayer, who started a Southern California treatment center, says it takes letting go of the ego in order to admit to having an illness. And, for some people, this is simply too hard to do. So he doesn't get hung up on terms like "illness" or "bipolar disorder." Instead, he focuses on helping people find appropriate treatment so that they can feel better and feel better about themselves. "Finding purpose and fulfillment is a constant evolution, and everyone struggles with it," Bayer tells Colby Itkowitz from the *Washington Post*. "[But] when people are the best versions of themselves, it feels amazing."

CHAPTER FOUR

Living with Bipolar Disorder

As a child, Natasha Tracy loved to have sleepovers. The problem was, she had ten times the energy that the other children had. By the end of the sleepover, the other kids and her mother were exhausted. No one could keep up with her. And then when the sleepover ended, she would cry and mope around the house.

Tracy writes in the *Daily Mail*:

When my friends came over, I would run around like a demon, elated they were there. I would want to stay up all night talking feverishly, long after my friends wanted to go

When she was young, Natasha Tracy loved to have sleepovers. But her bipolar disorder gave her ten times the energy of her friends and her mother. They could not keep up.

to sleep…And then I would beg my friends not to leave because I knew what would happen next. I knew that when they left I would feel down, sad, lonely, and depressed…It was like their leaving ripped out a part of my heart.

Despite Tracy's erratic moods, no one suspected that she had a mood disorder, let alone bipolar disorder.

In fact, she was simply labeled overly emotional even though her depressive episodes brought her to the brink of suicide more than once. For years, she struggled to make sense of her emotions and her moods. Eventually, she began self-harming, or cutting, as a way to cope with all of her negative feelings.

While in college, she began researching her symptoms and stumbled across some information on bipolar disorder. The information she found described her experiences exactly. But she was unwilling to admit that something might be that wrong—that she might have a lifelong illness. Doing so would require her to take medication for the rest of her life. That fact scared her.

Initially, doctors misdiagnosed her with mild depression. She was more than willing to accept this diagnosis because it meant not having to accept the larger truth—that she had bipolar disorder. After two years of trying different medications that failed to improve her moods, she was finally diagnosed with bipolar disorder.

She writes:

Life has not been easy since then. Several times my medication has lost its effectiveness...I've been hospitalized. … But still, things are better now… Getting a bipolar diagnosis was unimaginably scary, but it was a necessary part of getting better and getting my life back.

Acceptance Is the Key

For many people with bipolar disorder, accepting the fact that they have a mental illness can be the hardest part of treatment. No one wants to admit that something serious is wrong with him or her. It's the same reaction people have when they learn that they have heart disease or diabetes. To accept a diagnosis of bipolar disorder means they also must accept a complete lifestyle change. But experts say that acceptance is the first step in getting healthy.

"Accept that you have a condition that will sometimes affect your life in negative ways," says Karla Dougherty on Psych Central. Dougherty is an author who also has bipolar II disorder. "Accept that you cannot get rid of bipolar disorder the way you can get rid of the flu."

But, she adds, acceptance does not mean your life will lack meaning or that you must act like you are a victim. Many people with bipolar disorder have satisfying and fulfilling lives. Of course, anytime someone is diagnosed with bipolar disorder—or any other chronic condition—it's normal to experience some anxiety about how the illness will impact your life. Many times, these worries come from imagining worst-case scenarios. Try not to dwell on the what-ifs, but instead plan for them. In other words, think about what you want to have happen if you experience another manic episode or how you want to tackle thoughts of suicide.

Realize that you have some control over whether or not you get healthy or you get sicker. As a result, it is important not to ignore your illness or pretend like it doesn't exist. What this means is being vigilant about taking medications and keeping appointments with counselors and doctors.

Living Every Day with Bipolar Disorder

Living with bipolar disorder is not an easy task. After all, it is a lifelong illness that requires constant treatment. Yet, while there are emotional challenges, stigmas, and social challenges associated with bipolar disorder, many people with bipolar disorder live full and productive lives. The key is to change your lifestyle. Start by making healthy choices and taking care of yourself so that you can live symptom free. The first step is to stick to your treatment plan and to take your medication. And if you start to notice that it is not working effectively, contact someone on your health care team right away. It is not uncommon for medications to need to be changed or adjusted. Here are some other ideas for living a healthy lifestyle when you have bipolar disorder.

Reduce stress in your life. Typically, stress is a major trigger for people with bipolar disorder. As a result, it is important that you try to eliminate stress as much as possible. If you are in school, this may mean working with your teachers to create a workload that is manageable for you. For instance, because bipolar disorder is an illness that can impact learning, you may qualify for an Individualized Education Plan (IEP) that provides you with advance notice on assignments and extra time to complete tests.

Get plenty of sleep. Not getting enough sleep— even missing just a few hours of shut-eye—can be a trigger for people with bipolar disorder. It is important that you develop a consistent sleep schedule. The goal should be to go to bed at the same time every night. Remember, staying up late watching television or surfing the internet can worsen or trigger symptoms. So it is important to stay disciplined.

Incorporate exercise into your day. Ideally, you want to be exercising at least thirty minutes a day. This can be as simple as walking, running, or swimming or something more organized, like playing soccer, tennis, basketball, or any number of sports. The key is that you move around

Regular exercise is an important part of treating bipolar disorder because it helps to regulate moods. People with bipolar disorder should incorporate exercise into their treatment plan.

63

some every day. This movement will help keep your mood regulated.

Build a network of supportive people. For people with bipolar disorder, it is very important that they have a group of supportive people around them. There will be times when you will need extra help. Find a support group to talk with others about what you are experiencing. Others with bipolar disorder can provide suggestions and insights that those without the condition cannot.

Avoid using drugs and alcohol. Research has shown that drugs and alcohol can trigger an episode. So it is very important that people with bipolar disorder refrain from using any type of substance. These substances also can interfere with how medications work as well as disrupt sleep.

Pay attention to your symptoms. Even if you do everything right, you can still have a manic or a depressive episode. The key is to act quickly when you feel an episode beginning. Your doctor can help you even out your moods before they swing too far in one direction. Then, after an episode, be sure you take the time you need to recover.

How Can I Spot My Warning Signs?

When it comes to bipolar disorder, everyone is different. No two people have the same triggers or stressors. As a result, it is very important to know what things might impact your bipolar disorder or cause an episode. Try keeping a journal or a calendar where you track your moods as well as your activities. This exercise helps you learn more about yourself and what is normal for you and what isn't. It also can be useful in noticing triggers and stressors in your life.

For some people, an argument might be a trigger while for others it's a full schedule. Major life events, lack of sleep, and visiting certain locations also can be triggers. The key is to know what affects you. It's also important to learn how to recognize the onset of mania or depression so that you can get help right away. Be sure you talk to your family or friends so that they also can be on the lookout. Getting help right away when you start to experience an episode can help keep the

(continued on the next page)

(continued from the previous page)

situation manageable and under control. It also can help keep you and others around you safe.

Some possible signs that you might be experiencing a depressive episode include wanting to sleep all the time, feeling sad, empty, or tearful, or experiencing extensive guilt. You also might have significant changes in your appetite as well as difficulty concentrating or making decisions.

Meanwhile, some possible signs that you might be experiencing a manic episode include feeling overly energetic, having an inflated self-esteem, feeling invincible, and requiring less sleep than normal. Other symptoms might include talking fast or nonstop, having racing thoughts, being easily distracted, and excessively pursuing pleasure. As soon as you notice the first sign of a different mood, check in with your health care provider.

To Tell or Not to Tell About Your Illness

Telling people about your bipolar disorder is completely your choice. While it is essential to have a few trusted people in your corner to help you when things get challenging, it is not necessary to tell everyone you know that you have bipolar disorder. For the people who are closest to you, they may be relieved to learn that you have a diagnosis and that you are getting help. After all, it is highly likely that they have witnessed some of your episodes and knowing what is at the root could be a relief for them.

Meanwhile, other people who do not understand bipolar disorder or have the wrong ideas about the illness may not need to know at this point. Generally, it is best to tell only the people who can be helpful, empathetic, and encouraging about your illness. Unfortunately, there are many people who do not understand mood disorders. Instead, they feel you should be able to control your moods or just "snap out of it." This is simply not possible when it comes to bipolar disorder.

If you do decide to share your illness with people and they do not seem to understand what you are going through, be sure to share some pamphlets or other information. Even if they never change the way they think, remind yourself that getting treatment and sticking to your plan is the best thing

While it is important to tell a few trusted people about your illness, it is not necessary to tell everyone that you have bipolar disorder. Sharing this information is completely your choice.

you can do for yourself. And ignore any of the rude comments or jokes.

Handling Thoughts of Suicide

When it comes to bipolar disorder, suicide is a subject that cannot be ignored. In fact, some estimates indicate that nearly 30 percent of those diagnosed with bipolar disorder will attempt suicide at least once in their lives. In fact, according to the Depression and Bipolar Support Alliance (DBSA), bipolar disorder can reduce a person's life expectancy by 9.2 years. What's more, the suicide rate for people with bipolar disorder is nearly twenty times that of the general population.

For this reason, it is very important for people with bipolar disorder to have a plan in place in case they begin to feel suicidal. For instance, the DBSA suggests that you make a list of phone numbers of trusted friends, health care providers, and crisis hotlines that you can call when you are having trouble.

Remember that your life is important. Suicidal thoughts may be strong, but they are temporary and they are treatable symptoms of your illness. Get help when you start having these thoughts. You are worth it.

The DBSA also suggests making a Plan for Life. This plan begins with a promise you make to yourself to contact family members or friends anytime the thought of suicide enters your mind. And if you are unable to reach anyone, go to a hospital right away. Some other commitments they suggest that you make to yourself include:

- I will remind myself that my brain is lying to me and making things seem worse than they are. Suicidal thoughts are not based on reality, but are a symptom of my illness.
- I will remember that my life is valuable and worthwhile, even if it doesn't feel that way right now.
- I will stick with my prescribed treatment plan and remember to take my medications.
- I will stay aware of my moods, know my warning signs, and get help early.

Having suicidal thoughts happens to a lot of people with bipolar disorder. The key is to recognize that suicidal thoughts are often a sign that you want to end the pain that bipolar disorder causes you, not that you truly want to end your life. In fact, once you recognize that these thoughts are related to your illness, you can counteract them with realistic thoughts.

Many people with bipolar disorder will have suicidal thoughts. It is important to know whom to call for help and support when those thoughts creep in. Keep this info nearby and handy.

Another way to counteract the risk of having suicidal thoughts is by sticking to your treatment plan. Doing so can reduce your suicidal thoughts significantly. Remember, bipolar disorder is an illness. As a result, you need to take your medication and get help when things seem to be getting worse.

If you had the flu and thought you might die from it, you would go to the hospital or a doctor. The same is true with bipolar disorder. You need to call your doctor and get help for your illness. Remember, there is no shame in asking for help from other people. It does not make you weak. In fact, it takes a lot of courage to ask for help.

"Suffering from any kind of mental illness is a constant struggle, a constant battle," writes J. B. Burrage for Bipolar Hope, an online resource for people with bipolar disorder. "We're trying to stay above water. Sometimes we succeed but other [times], it's really hard to do without someone throwing out a life raft."

10 Great Questions to Ask Your Doctor

1. How is bipolar disorder managed?

2. What medications are you prescribing?

3. What are the side effects?

4. What happens if the medication does not work?

5. Aside from medication, what else should my treatment plan include?

6. How often will I see you and the others on my treatment team?

7. How do I make sure that my bipolar disorder is managed well?

8. Where can I find support for my bipolar disorder?

9. What do I do if I notice the warning signs of mania or depression?

10. What suggestions do you have for living with bipolar disorder?

CHAPTER FIVE

How to Help a Friend or Family Member with Bipolar Disorder

Impulsive, high-strung, and wildly emotional—her family affectionately nicknamed her T. Rex when she was little. They thought her stormy emotions were cute, and even humorous at times, recalls her sister, Grace Smollen* in *O Magazine*. But as Smollen's sister grew older, her moods and emotions spiraled out of control, turning from an "occasional thundercloud into a Category 5 hurricane most days," she writes. Trying to determine what was at the root of the emotional turmoil was not an easy process. And, in the end, it was draining on the family.

Smollen writes:

The attempt to diagnose my sister was a... frustrating business, The labels—ADHD, depression, anxiety, bipolar—seemed to identify the symptoms, but never offered a solution. There were always new meds, new therapists, new doctors. In her teen years, there were suicide attempts—threatened and actual, both equally catastrophic to those who loved her.

When Smollen left for college, hundreds of miles from home, she felt relieved to be away from the chaos. She knew she was the lucky one. After all, she was able to be independent and in control of her life, unlike her sister. But, even though she was far from home, she was not able to completely escape the hold her sister's mental illness had on her family.

Smollen writes:

I kept being drawn into the drama of her disease, my parents' despair bubbling over in late-night phone calls to me when they needed support. And I couldn't deny feeling resentful when I saw all our family's resources—time, love, attention, money—going to her.

Today, Smollen's sister seems to be effectively managing her illness. No longer does her mother arrange the seven pills she takes daily to manage

Living with a person impacted by bipolar disorder can be hard, but it is important for family members to remember they can have a positive impact by learning about the illness.

her moods. She instead takes responsibility for this chore on her own. And Smollen is finally able to let her guard down and truly get to know her sister.

"I felt it was safe, finally, to get to know her," she writes. "Because of the pain she'd endured, my sister was compassionate when the heart and mind were unaligned."

Living with a Bipolar Family Member

Much like Smollen's story, living with a person who has been diagnosed with bipolar disorder can be hard.

The illness is not only confusing and frustrating, but it also can leave family members feeling helpless and uncertain of where to turn. At times, it may even feel like it is sucking the life out of the relationship.

But it doesn't have to be this way. You have the power to have a positive impact on your friend or family member. In fact, the first thing you should do is learn everything you can about bipolar disorder. Being educated about the illness will help you make informed decisions about how best to support your loved one.

It's also important to remember that bipolar disorder is a treatable illness that affects a person's brain. It is a real illness, just like diabetes, heart disease, or asthma, and is not a character flaw or personal weakness. It also is not caused by anything you or your family did. Likewise, you cannot cure the person with bipolar disorder and you certainly cannot fix your loved one's problems. But you can offer your love, support, and understanding. Too many times, family members and friends focus on the illness instead of the person. Remember, your loved one is not defined by his or her illness. He or she is a real person struggling with an illness that he or she cannot control.

Family members can feel guilty if things in their lives are going well while a loved one is struggling with bipolar disorder. But they can live a normal life and support their loved one, too.

Making Sense of Your Feelings

It can feel overwhelming when you discover that someone you love has bipolar disorder. It is not uncommon to struggle with a wide range of feelings. Initially, you may deny that there is anything wrong, but eventually you will have to face the fact that your friend or family member has a mental illness.

Once you reach this point, it is normal to experience a sense of loss. You will grieve over the loss of your hopes and dreams. You may even struggle with letting go. But you have to let go of any idea that you can heal your loved one. Bipolar disorder is a treatable illness, but it is not curable.

You also may struggle with feeling guilty, especially when your life is going well or you feel happy. It can be hard to watch a friend or family member struggle when things in your life seem to fall into place. You also may minimize your hardships or challenges because you feel that what you are experiencing is nothing in comparison to what he or she is going through. But the truth is you matter, too. You cannot allow the illness to consume your life. Never give it that much control. You need to focus on the person, not the disease.

Take Care of Yourself

Bipolar disorder is exhausting. It can sap your energy and steal your happiness if you let it. As a result, it is very important that you take care of yourself. You cannot be calm, loving, patient, or gentle when all of your mental and physical strength is gone. What's more, you don't have to be available to your friend or family member twenty-four hours a day. It's perfectly normal, and even encouraged, that you take time for yourself. Make sure you still do the things you enjoy—the things that nourish you and recharge your batteries. This might mean going for a walk, seeing a movie with friends, reading a good book, or going on a mini trip. Trying to be everything and do everything for your loved one is impossible, and it is not really helpful.

People with bipolar disorder need to learn to be independent and take care of themselves. They need your support, your love, and your encouragement, but they do not need you to do things that they could do for themselves. Putting yourself in the role of caretaker will slow down their progress. What's more, it is not uncommon for people with bipolar disorder to fall into victim thinking. When this happens, they will not take responsibility for their actions and expect to be given a pass every time they hurt someone. For this reason, it is very important that you set boundaries with your loved one.

Knowing the Difference Between a Mood Disorder and a Mood Swing

When it comes to differentiating between a mood disorder and an ordinary mood swing, it helps to look at the intensity, the length, and the interference with life. Here is an overview of the common differences.

- A mood disorder is usually more severe or dramatic than a mood swing.
- Typically, an ordinary mood swing is gone within a few hours or may even last a day or so. But mania or depression can last weeks or months at a time. Meanwhile, if someone is rapid cycling, his or her high and low moods can come and go quickly, but the person does not have a stable mood for a long period of time.
- Extreme moods caused by bipolar disorder can cause serious problems. For instance, someone with depression may not be able to get out of bed while a person experiencing mania might go days without sleep or spend money she does not have.

Setting Boundaries with Your Friend or Family Member

When you set boundaries with a friend or family member, you are letting him or her know how you want to be treated, which is a vital part of taking care of yourself. It is an important part of living with someone who suffers from bipolar disorder. Just be sure you are honest about your expectations without hurting or blowing up at the person in the process. Remember, you have the right to protect and defend yourself. But you should do so in a calm and respectful manner. Ultimately, setting boundaries will improve your relationship with your loved one or family member because everyone understands what is expected.

Keep in mind that the whole point of setting boundaries is to improve the relationship—not control it. If done properly, setting boundaries will not separate you from your loved one but will instead enable you to coexist peacefully. There are times, though, when setting boundaries will end the relationship. If this happens, it is important to remember that your emotional and physical health is important, too. Allowing someone to take advantage of you, physically hurt you, or wound you emotionally is not healthy. So you may have to let the friendship go in order to protect yourself.

Steps to Setting Effective Boundaries

The first step in setting boundaries is to let your loved one know what it is that you find unacceptable. For instance, does your loved one borrow money and not repay it? Does he say mean things? Be very direct about what bothers you. Proper boundaries call out a specific behavior or behaviors that you want to change.

After you have mentioned the behavior, you should talk about how it makes you feel. For instance, you might say, "I feel hurt and scared when you yell at me." A good boundary will identify what your expectations are. It is important that you be very direct about what you want. For example, you might say, "I expect you to treat me respectfully, especially after I tell you that your words are hurting my feelings."

Doctors Sometimes Discriminate Against the Mentally Ill

According to the *New York Times*, at least fourteen studies have shown that patients with a serious mental illness receive worse medical care than mentally healthy people. In fact, in 2012 the World Health Organization called the stigma and discrimination people with mental illnesses experience "a hidden human rights emergency." When doctors discriminate in this way, it is called diagnostic overshadowing. And it happens a lot, writes Juliann Garey. What's more, she says that people who suffer from a serious mental illness and use the public health care system die twenty-five years earlier than those without one. She writes:

True, suicide is a big factor, accounting for 30 to 40 percent of early deaths. But 60 percent die of preventable or treatable conditions. First on the list is, unsurprisingly, cardiovascular disease. Two studies showed that patients with both a mental illness and a cardiovascular condition received about half the number of follow-up interventions, like bypass surgery or cardia catheterization, after having a heart attack than did the "normal" cardiac patients.

Garey, who has bipolar disorder, says she has received this type of mistreatment by doctors on more than one occasion. In fact, one time an ear, nose, and throat doctor refused to prescribe anything for an ear infection. The next day, her eardrum ruptured, leaving her with minor hearing loss.

This type of treatment happens all the time to people with bipolar disorder. But there are changes being made as efforts to educate people about mental illness become more prominent. In fact, Columbia University now offers a program called narrative medicine. The goal is to look beyond the chart and to the person.

Spell out the consequences for crossing the line. For instance, you could say, "If you continue to treat me disrespectfully after I have asked you not to, I will end the conversation and leave the room. We will not continue our conversation until you can recognize how you hurt me and can talk to me respectfully."

7 Things to Remember About Bipolar Disorder

1. Your loved one's behavior may change from day to day. Be prepared for those changes.
2. Your loved one's improvement will take time, especially until the right medications are found. So it may not be easy to see change on a day-to-day basis. Be patient.
3. Your loved one needs to learn to be self-reliant. Expect appropriate behavior and avoid rushing in and doing things for him or her that he or she could do himself or herself. Be supportive.
4. Your loved one needs you to be positive and forgiving. Avoid saying words like "never" and "always" when your loved one repeats past mistakes. Be encouraging.
5. Your loved one needs stability. Keep your promises so that your loved one knows you can be counted on. Be reliable.
6. Your loved one may need space. Avoid constant monitoring and check-ins. Not only could this increase stress and cause an

episode, but it is also not allowing your loved one to become independent. Be empowering.

7. Your loved one is not defined by bipolar disorder. There is a person there with all kinds of feelings and emotions. Refrain from attributing everything to the illness. It is dehumanizing. Be a friend.

Never define a loved one by her illness. She is still a person with feelings and needs to be treated with love and kindness. There is so much more to people than a diagnosis.

Make sure you do not threaten the person or try to control him or her in some way. Simply state how you expect to be treated and what you will do in response to his or her hurtful behaviors. And, finally, enforce your boundaries. If you do not enforce your boundaries by following through on the consequences, then you have wasted your time in putting them out there. Additionally, there is no motivation for your loved one to treat you more respectfully.

What You Can Do to Support Your Friend or Family Member

One of the most challenging aspects of bipolar disorder is how unpredictable the illness can be. You can sometimes feel like you are always on guard, waiting for something bad to happen. Or you may spend a lot of time worrying that your loved one is going to have another out-of-control manic episode, become suicidal during a depressive episode, or need to be hospitalized again. As a result, it is normal to feel like you have no control over the situation.

While it is true that you cannot control the disease or your loved one, you can do things to support your friend or family member that empower you and give you a sense of purpose in his or her journey. Here are some things you can do to support your friend or loved one.

Be understanding and forgiving. It is not uncommon for a person with bipolar disorder to act out in ways that are hurtful to others during an episode. Try to remember that your loved one does not want to hurt you or others. While he or she should take responsibility for his or her actions and make amends, remind yourself that it was the illness causing his or her brain to make bad choices. It is important to be understanding and forgiving. However, if his or her hurtful behavior was due to refusing treatment or not taking medications, he or she needs to recognize the damage he or she has done. While it is important to be forgiving, you also can hold him or her accountable. Stress the importance of sticking to the treatment plan and following up with health care providers when it doesn't seem to be working. You also may need strong boundaries if your loved one continues to refuse treatment.

Be aware of mood changes. While you do not need to monitor everything your loved one does, if you do notice that he or she is isolating more or suddenly has a lot of energy, bring this to his or her attention. If he or she is unwilling to listen or seek medical treatment, be prepared to get him or her the medical help he or she needs. Sometimes, people with bipolar disorder enjoy the increased energy they experience during a manic episode, so they will put off getting treatment. It is important to intervene by calling their health care team before things get out of hand. It is much better for your loved one to have stabilized moods than it is to be cycling in and out of the highs and lows of bipolar disorder.

Become an advocate. As someone who sees your friend or family member on a regular basis, you have firsthand knowledge about what is taking place in his or her life. As a result, you can fill in the blanks for health care professionals if your friend or family member is open to this. Your insight can be very helpful. You have seen him or her on good days and on bad days. You know what works for him or her and what doesn't. Don't be afraid to share that information when asked.

You also can become an advocate by speaking out about mental illness and trying to dispel some of the myths surrounding it. Educate people on what it

Remember that bipolar disorder is the enemy here, not your friend. Do what you can to be supportive because with proper and consistent treatment your friend can live a happy life.

means to have bipolar disorder. Doing so can help your friend or family member immensely. Some of the biggest challenges people with bipolar disorder face are the misconceptions about what it means to have a mental illness. If you help educate the people around them, you are creating a safe space for them to get better.

Remember that the disease is the enemy. When supporting a friend or family member with a mental illness, it is important to remind yourself that the disease is the enemy not your loved one. Encourage him or her to fight the disease by taking his or her medications and following his or her treatment plan. Remind him or her that you are there for him or her and that you understand that he or she is suffering. But your loved one can overcome this and live a healthy, productive life.

anticonvulsants Drugs that are usually used to treat seizure disorders.

antipsychotics Drugs that are sometimes used on a short-term basis to treat bipolar disorder; they control symptoms like mania, delusions, and hallucinations.

anxiolytics Antianxiety medications used to treat anxiety and panic disorders.

bipolar disorder A mental illness or mood disorder in which the person experiences periods of mania and depression.

cholesterol A waxy substance found in your body used to make hormones and to allow your body to function; high levels of cholesterol are unhealthy.

cyclothymia A mild mood disorder that is similar to bipolar disorder but the highs and lows do not reach extreme levels.

depressive episode A period of low mood or depression that occurs in people with bipolar disorder.

diabetes A chronic illness in which a person's body does not produce or respond to the hormone insulin.

diagnostic overshadowing Occurs when a health care professional wrongly assumes that a person's physical symptoms are a consequence of the person's mental illness; when this happens the person with a mental illness does not receive appropriate treatment.

dual diagnosis A term used when a person is diagnosed with a mental illness and a substance abuse disorder.

gold standard A term used in the medical field to describe the best type of treatment or test for a particular condition.

hypomania A mild form of mania that people with bipolar II disorder experience.

lithium A naturally occurring salt used to treat bipolar disorder; it is considered the gold standard for treatment.

mania An elevated mood that people with bipolar disorder experience; it can lead to impulsivity, irritability, overactivity, sleeplessness, delusions, and more.

manic episode A mood state that people with bipolar disorder may experience; it lasts at least one week and is characterized by an elevated mood or euphoria.

mental illness A health condition that causes changes in mood, thinking, or behavior.

mixed episode When a person with bipolar disorder experiences symptoms of both mania and depression within a single episode.

neurotransmitters Often referred to as the body's chemical messengers.

predisposition The likelihood that someone will experience a mental illness based on genetic, environmental, and heritable factors.

schizophrenia A long-term mental illness in which the person experiences a breakdown between thoughts, emotions, and behaviors; this breakdown leads to inappropriate actions and feelings as well as flawed perceptions and an inability to see reality.

serotonin A chemical and neurotransmitter that is found in the body; it helps regulate mood, behavior, sleep, and more.

talk therapy The process a psychologist uses to help people learn how to understand and cope with problems they are facing.

unipolar depression A depressed mood lasting for at least two weeks that does not include any periods of mania or elevated mood.

For More Information

Canadian Mental Health Association
250 Dundas Street West, Suite 500
Toronto, OH M5T 2Z5
(416) 646-5557
Website: https://cmha.ca
Twitter: @CMHA_NTL
Instagram: @cmhanational
The Canadian Mental Health Association
   is dedicated to improving the public's
   understanding of mental health issues. They
   provide resources that allow people to maintain
   and improve their mental health and work
   within the community to build resilience and
   support recovery from mental illness.

Depression and Bipolar Support Alliance
55 E. Jackson Boulevard, Suite 490
Chicago, IL 60604
(800) 826-3632
Website: http://www.dbsalliance.org
Facebook and Twitter: @DBSAlliance
The Depression and Bipolar Support Alliance
   is dedicated to helping people with mood
   disorders manage their lives. Their goals are to

support, educate, and bring hope to the lives of people with depression and bipolar disorder.

Here to Help (Canada)
905-1130 West Pender Street
Vancouver, BC V6E 4A4
(800) 661-2121
Website: http://www.heretohelp.bc.ca
Twitter: @HeretoHelpBC
Here to Help is a project of the BC Partners for
    Mental Health and Substance Use Information.
    As a group of seven nonprofit agencies
    dedicated to mental health and addiction
    recovery, they work together to help people live
    healthier lives while preventing and managing
    mental health and substance use issues.

International Bipolar Foundation (IBPF)
8775 Aero Drive, Suite 330
San Diego, CA 92123
(858) 598-5967
Website: http://ibpf.org
Facebook: @InternationalBipolarFoundation
Twitter: @@IntlBipolar

IBPF is a nonprofit organization designed to
improve the understanding and treatment
of bipolar disorder through research. They
also strive to remove the stigma surrounding
bipolar disorder through educational programs.
In addition, they provide resources and
information for people with the illness as well as
those who care for them.

Mental Health America
2000 N. Beauregard Street, 6th Floor
Alexandria, VA 22311
(800) 969-6642
Website: http://www.nmha.org
Twitter: @mentalhealtham
Facebook and Instagram: @mentalhealthamerica
This nonprofit mental health association is
dedicated to helping people with mental illness
find the help they need. They assist both the
person with the illness and their families in
finding treatment, support groups, details about
medications, and information about financial
issues related to treatment.

National Alliance on Mental Illness (NAMI)
3803 N. Fairfax Drive, Suite 100
Arlington, VA 22203
(703) 524-7600
Website: https://www.nami.org
Facebook: @NAMI
Instagram and Twitter: @NAMICommunicate
As the nation's largest grassroots mental health
    organization, NAMI is dedicated to improving
    the lives of the millions of Americans impacted
    by mental illness. They work to shape public
    policy as well as provide educational tools
    and resources for those with mental illness
    and their families.

National Institute of Mental Health (NIMH)
6001 Executive Boulevard
Room 6200, MSC 9663
Bethesda, MD 20892-9663
(301) 443-4513
Website: http://www.nimh.nih.gov
Facebook and Twitter: @nimhgov
Part of the US Department of Health and Human
    Services, NIMH is the top federal agency for

research on mental disorders. What's more, the NIMH is one of twenty-seven institutes that comprise the National Institutes of Health, the largest biomedical research agency in the world.

For Further Reading

Kandel, Eric. *The Disordered Mind: What Unusual Brains Tell Us About Ourselves*. New York, NY: Farrar, Straus and Giroux, 2018.

Landau, Jennifer. *Bipolar Disorder* (Teen Mental Health). New York, NY: Rosen Publishing Group, 2014.

Leonard, Basia, and Joann Jovinelly. *Bipolar Disorder: Understanding Brain Diseases and Disorders*. New York, NY: Rosen Publishing Group, 2012.

Letran, Jacqui. *I Would but My Damn Mind Won't Let Me*. Healed Mind, LLC, 2016.

Niven, Jennifer. *All the Bright Places*. New York, NY: Knopf, 2015.

Peters, Elisa, and Hope Killcoyne. *Psychology: The Britannica Guide to Social Sciences*. New York, NY: Rosen Publishing Group, 2016.

Sedley, Ben. *Stuff That Sucks: A Teen's Guide to Accepting What You Can't Change and Committing to What You Can*. Oakland, CA: Instant Help, 2017.

Spilsbury, Richard. *Bipolar Disorder: Gene Diseases and Gene Therapies*. New York, NY: Rosen Publishing Group, 2019.

Toner, Jacqueline. *Depression: A Teen's Guide to Survive and Thrive*. Washington, DC: Magination Press, 2016.

Bibliography

Addiction Center. "Understanding Bipolar Disorder." Retrieved September 19, 2018. https://www.addictioncenter.com/addiction /bipolar-disorder.

Barnett, Jennifer H., and Jordan W. Smoller. "The Gentics of Bipolar Disorder." *Neuroscience,* April 27, 2013. https://www.ncbi.nlm.nih.gov/pmc /articles/PMC3637882.

Bromwich, Jonah Engle. "Mariah Carey Opens Up About Bipolar Disorder." *New York Times*, April 11, 2018. https://www.nytimes.com/2018/04/11 /style/mariah-carey-bipolar-disorder.html.

Burrage, JB. "Demi Lovato and Why We Can't Forget Our Own Bipolar Disorder Battles." BP Hope, September 4, 2018. https://www.bphope .com/blog/demi-lovato-and-the-struggle-of -being-a-face-of-bipolar-disorder.

Cagle, Jess. "Mariah Carey: My Battle with Bipolar Disorder." *People*, April 11, 2018. https://people .com/music/mariah-carey-bipolar-disorder -diagnosis-exclusive.

Cagle, Jess. "Mariah Carey on Why She Kept Her Bipolar Disorder Hidden for Years." *People*, April 11, 2018. https://people.com/music

/mariah-carey-bipolar-disorder-why-hide
-denial-isolation.

Conversation, The. "Gene-based Tests May
Improve Treatment for People with Bipolar
Disorder." April 3, 2018. https://theconversation
.com/gene-based-tests-may-improve-treatment
-for-people-with-bipolar-disorder-87680.

Davies, Madlen. "The Moment I Realized I Have
Bipolar Disorder." *Daily Mail*, October 9, 2015.
https://www.dailymail.co.uk/health
/article-3265278/The-moment-realised-bipolar
-disorder-One-woman-s-candid-story-living
-condition-pushed-self-harm-consider-suicide
.html.

Depression and Bipolar Support Alliance. "Bipolar
Disorder Statistics." Retrieved September 24,
2018. https://secure2.convio.net/dabsa/site
/SPageServer/?pagename=education
_statistics_bipolar_disorder.

Depression and Bipolar Support Alliance. "You've
Just Been Diagnosed…" Retrieved September
24, 2018. https://secure2.convio.net/dabsa/site
/SPageServer/?pagename=education
_brochures_just_diagnosed.

Doheny, Kathleen. "8 Myths About Bipolar Disorder." WebMD. https://www.webmd.com /bipolar-disorder/features/8-myths-about -bipolar-disorder#1.

Fast, Julie. "Loving Someone with Bipolar Disorder." Bipolar Happens. October 9, 2016. http://www.bipolarhappens.com/bhblog/loving -someone-with-bipolar-disorder.

Fink, Candida, and Joe Kraynak. *Bipolar Disorder for Dummies*. Hoboken, NJ: John Wiley & Sons, Inc.,. 2016.

Garey, Juliann. "When Doctors Discriminate." *New York Times*, August 10, 2013. https://www .nytimes.com/2013/08/11/opinion/sunday /when-doctors-discriminate.html.

HealthLine. "In Their Shoes: Understanding What Bipolar Disorder Feels Like." Retrieved September 14, 2018. https://www .healthline.com/health/bipolar-disorder/what -bipolar-feels-like#1.

HealthyPlace. "When a Close Friend Has a Mental Illness." April 7, 2017. https://www.healthyplace .com/bipolar-disorder/articles/when-someone -close-to-you-has-a-mental-illness.

Heiser, Christina. "Demi Lovato Speaks Up About Living with Bipolar Disorder." *Women's Health*, May 28, 2015. https://www.womenshealthmag .com/health/a19925262/demi-lovato-be-vocal -campaign.

Itkowitz, Colby. "Demi Lovato Lives with Bipolar Disorder. Before Every Concert She Holds Mental Health Workshops for Fans." *Washington Post,* June 27, 2016. https://www .washingtonpost.com/news/inspired-life/wp /2016/07/27/demi-lovato-lives-with-bipolar -disorder-before-every-concert-she-holds -mental-health-workshops-for-fans/?utm _term=.5906ba0ed40e.

Johnston, Janice. "Demi Lovato's Shocking Diagnosis." ABC News, April 21, 2011. https:// abcnews.go.com/Entertainment/demi-lovatos -shocking-diagnosis-bipolar-disorder /story?id=13426303.

Kalustian, Caitlyn. "When You're Sitting in the Aftermath of a Bipolar Episode." The Mighty, December 8, 2017. https://themighty .com/2017/12/just-came-out-of-bipolar -depressive-manic-episode.

Mazziotta, Julie. "Mariah Carey Reveals Her Mental Health Struggle: What to Know About Bipolar II Disorder." *People*, April 11, 2018. https://people.com/health/what-is-bipolar-ii-disorder.

Michael, April. "Why Bipolar Disorder Is So Hard to Diagnose and What You Can Do About It." BP Hope, July 25, 2017. https://www.bphope.com/blog/why-bipolar-disorder-in-adults-is-so-hard-to-diagnose-and-what-you-can-do-about-it.

National Institute of Mental Health. "Bipolar Disorder." April 2016. https://www.nimh.nih.gov/health/topics/bipolar-disorder/index.shtml.

Purse, Marcia. "What Is Bipolar Disorder Not Otherwise Specified." Verywell Mind, June 28, 2018. https://www.verywellmind.com/diagnosing-bipolar-disorder-not-otherwise-specified-379952.

Read, Kimberly. "Warning Signs of Suicide in Bipolar Patients." Verywell Mind, July 14, 2018. https://www.verywellmind.com/red-flags-warning-signs-of-suicide-379034.

Roberts, Dawna. "How Families Can Support Their Loved Ones Living with Bipolar Disorder."

Families for Depression Awareness, December 22, 2017. http://www.familyaware.org/caregiver-to-caregiver-bd-support.

Smollen, Grace*. "What It Was Like Growing Up with a Sibling Afflicted with Bipolar Disorder." *Oprah*. Retrieved September 24, 2018. http://www.oprah.com/inspiration/what-it-was-like-growing-up-with-a-mentally-ill-sister. *author's name has been changed

Tartakovsky, Margarite "Bipolar Disorder: When You Feel Like You're Starting Over." PsychCentral. Retrieved October 19, 2018. https://psychcentral.com/blog/bipolar-disorder-when-you-feel-like-youre-starting-over.

Thomas, Jennifer. "The Challenge of Accurately Diagnosing Bipolar Disorder." *Health*, February 29, 2016. https://www.health.com/health/condition-article/0,,20275016,00.html.

WebMD. "Understanding Bipolar Disorder." October 15, 2016. https://www.webmd.com/bipolar-disorder/understanding-bipolar-disorder#1.

Weiss, Suzannah. "Demi Lovato Explains Why You Shouldn't Call Her Bipolar." *Teen Vogue*, August

2, 2017. https://www.teenvogue.com/story
/demi-lovato-label-bipolar.

Worth, Tammy. "10 Subtle Signs of Bipolar
Disorder." *Health*, February 27, 2012. https://
www.health.com/health/gallery/0,,20436786,00
.html.

Index

A

Addiction Center, 38
ADHD, 17, 74
alcohol abuse, 38, 64
anticonvulsants, 52
antidepressants, 54–55
antipsychotics, 52
anxiety, 17
anxiolytics, 55–56

B

Bearden, Carrie, 31, 35, 38
Be Vocal, 14
Bipolar Happens, 29
Bipolar Hope, 17, 72
bipolar I, 15–16
bipolar II, 16
borderline personality disorder, 17
brain functions, 37–39
Burrage, JB, 72

C

Carey, Mariah, 27–29
causes, 36–40
Churchill, Winston, 4
comorbidity, 17
cyclothymic disorder, 16

D

denial, 29–31
depakote, 52
Depression and Bipolar Support Alliance (DBSA), 4, 69
depressive episodes, 22–23, 34–36
diabetes, 6, 52, 60, 77
diagnosis, 17–19
diagnostic overshadowing, 84
discrimination, 84–85
Dougherty, Karla, 60
drug abuse, 38, 64
dual diagnosis, 30

E

eating disorders, 17
education, 48
environmental factors, 40
exercise, 63–64

About the Author

Sherri Mabry Gordon is a bullying prevention advocate, health and parenting writer, and author of numerous nonfiction books. Many of her books deal with issues teens face today, including bullying, abuse, public shaming, online safety, and more. Gordon also writes about bullying, relationships, and health issues for VerywellFamily.com. She has given multiple presentations to schools, churches, and the YMCA on bullying prevention, dating abuse, and online safety and volunteers regularly. She also serves on the School Counselor Advisory Board for two schools. Gordon resides in Columbus, Ohio, with her husband, two children, and a dog.

Photo Credits

Cover pixelfit/E+/Getty Images; p. 5 Mondadori Portfolio/Getty Images; p. 6 Everett Historical/Shutterstock.com; p. 7 fstop123/iStock/Getty Images; p. 10 Isabel Infantes/PA Images/Getty Images; p. 11 Amanda Edwards/WireImage/Getty Images; p. 19 asiseeit/E+/Getty Images; p. 21 Merla/Shutterstock.com; p. 23 Lopolo/Shutterstock.com; p. 28 Everett Collection/Shutterstock.com; p. 33 ESB Professional/Shutterstock.com; p. 36 Juanmonino/iStock/Getty Images; p. 39 Daisy Daisy/Shutterstock.com; p. 44 Steve Debenport/E+/Getty Images; p. 47 © iStockphoto/KatarzynaBialasiewicz; p. 50 aastock/Shutterstock.com; p. 58 Reggie Casagrande/Photolibrary/Getty Images; p. 63 Westend61/Getty Images; p. 68 Corbis/VCG/Getty Images; p. 71 National Suicide Prevention Lifeline; p. 76 silverkblackstock/Shutterstock.com; p. 78 XiXinXing/Shutterstock.com; p. 87 Antonio Guillem/Shutterstock.com; p. 91 Iryna Inshyna/Shutterstock.com.

Design and Layout: Nicole Russo-Duca; Editor: Elissa Petruzzi; Photo Researcher: Sherri Jackson